ANTHOLOGY

NURSERY RHYMES

SELECTED BY SALLY EMERSON

ILLUSTRATED BY MOIRA & COLIN MACLEAN

Kingfisher Books

Kingfisher Books, Grisewood & Dempsey Ltd,
Elsley House, 24–30 Great Titchfield Street, London W1P 7AD

First published in 1992 by Kingfisher Books.
10 9 8 7 6 5 4 3 2 1
The material in this edition was previously published by Kingfisher Books in
The Kingfisher Nursery Treasury (1988)
and *The Kingfisher Nursery Songbook* (1991).

British Library Cataloguing-in-Publication Data
A catalogue record for this book is available from the British Library

ISBN 0 86272 888 6

Phototypeset by Southern Positives and Negatives (SPAN), Lingfield, Surrey
Printed and bound in Spain

CONTENTS

Humpty Dumpty sat on a wall,
Humpty Dumpty had a great fall;
    All the King's horses,
    And all the King's men,
Couldn't put Humpty together again.

Old King Cole was a merry old soul,
And a merry old soul was he;
   He called for his pipe,
    And he called for his bowl,
And he called for his fiddlers three.

Every fiddler he had a fiddle,
And a very fine fiddle had he;
   Oh, there's none so rare
    As can compare
With King Cole and his fiddlers three.

It's raining, it's pouring,
The old man's snoring;
He got into bed
and bumped his head
And he couldn't get up in the morning.

Doctor Foster went to Gloucester
In a shower of rain;
He stepped in a puddle,
Right up to his middle,
And never went there again.

One misty, moisty morning,
When cloudy was the weather,
I met a little old man
Clothed all in leather.

He began to compliment,
And I began to grin,
How do you do, and how do you do,
And how do you do again?

Oh, do you know the muffin man,
The muffin man, the muffin man,
Oh, do you know the muffin man
Who lives in Drury Lane?

Polly put the kettle on,
Polly put the kettle on,
Polly put the kettle on,
 We'll all have tea.

Sukey take it off again,
Sukey take it off again,
Sukey take it off again,
 They've all gone away.

Hot cross buns! Hot cross buns!
One a penny, two a penny,
 hot cross buns.
If you have no daughters,
Give them to your sons.
One a penny, two a penny,
 hot cross buns.

7

Rain, rain, go away,
Come again another day,
All the children want to play.
Rain, rain, go to Spain,
Never show your face again.

Rub-a-dub-dub,
Three men in a tub,
And who do you think they be?
The butcher, the baker,
The candlestick-maker;
Turn 'em out, knaves all three!

Pease porridge hot,
Pease porridge cold,
Pease porridge in the pot,
Nine days old.
Some like it hot,
Some like it cold,
Some like it in the pot,
Nine days old.

Jack Sprat could eat no fat,
His wife could eat no lean,
And so between them both, you see,
They licked the platter clean.

Little Boy Blue,
   Come blow your horn.
The sheep's in the meadow,
   The cow's in the corn.
Where is the boy
   Who looks after the sheep?
He's under a haystack
   Fast asleep.
Will you wake him?
   No, not I,
For if I do,
   He's sure to cry.

Ladybird, ladybird,
   Fly away home,
Your house is on fire
   Your children all gone;
All but one,
   And her name is Ann,
And she has crept under
   The warming pan.

Lavender's blue, dilly, dilly,
　Lavender's green;
When I am king, dilly, dilly,
　You shall be queen.

Call up your men, dilly, dilly,
　Set them to work,
Some to the plough, dilly, dilly,
　Some to the cart.

Some to make hay, dilly, dilly,
　Some to thresh corn,
Whilst you and I, dilly, dilly,
　Keep ourselves warm.

Three blind mice! Three blind mice!
See how they run! See how they run!
They all ran after the farmer's wife,
Who cut off their tails with a carving knife;
Did you ever see such a thing in your life,
   As three blind mice?

Hickory, dickory, dock,
The mouse ran up the clock.
  The clock struck one,
  The mouse ran down,
Hickory, dickory, dock.

Ding, dong, bell,
Pussy's in the well.
Who put her in?
    Little Johnny Green.
Who pulled her out?
    Little Tommy Stout.
What a naughty boy was that
To try to drown poor pussy cat,
Who never did him any harm,
But killed the mice in his father's barn.

I love little pussy,
    Her coat is so warm,
And if I don't hurt her
    She'll do me no harm.

So I'll not pull her tail,
    Nor drive her away,
But pussy and I
    Very gently will play.

She shall sit by my side,
    And I'll give her some food;
And pussy will love me
    Because I am good.

13

There was a little girl,
And she had a little curl
Right in the middle of her forehead;
When she was good,
She was very, very good,
But when she was bad,
She was horrid.

Tom, Tom, the piper's son,
Stole a pig and away he run;
The pig was eat,
And Tom was beat,
And Tom went howling
Down the street.

Georgie Porgie, pudding and pie,
Kissed the girls and made them cry.
When the boys came out to play,
Georgie Porgie ran away.

Girls and boys, come out to play,
The moon doth shine as bright as day.
Leave your supper and leave your sleep,
And come with your playfellows into the street.
Come with a whoop and come with a call,
Come with a good will or not at all.
Up the ladder and down the wall,
A half-penny loaf will serve us all;
You find milk, and I'll find flour,
And we'll have a pudding in half an hour.

Goosey, goosey gander,
  Whither shall I wander?
Upstairs and downstairs
  And in my lady's chamber.
There I met an old man
  Who would not say his prayers,
I took him by the left leg
  And threw him down the stairs.

Hickety, pickety, my black hen,
She lays eggs for gentlemen;

Sometimes one, and sometimes ten,
Hickety, pickety, my black hen.

Up and down the City Road,
  In and out the Eagle,
That's the way the money goes,
  Pop goes the weasel!

Half a pound of tuppenny rice,
  Half a pound of treacle,
Mix it up and make it nice,
  Pop goes the weasel!

Yankee Doodle came to town,
    Riding on a pony;
He stuck a feather in his cap
    And called it macaroni.

First he bought a porridge pot,
    And then he bought a ladle,
And then he trotted home again
    As fast as he was able.

Bobby Shaftoe's gone to sea,
Silver buckles on his knee;
He'll come back and marry me,
    Bonny Bobby Shaftoe.

Bobby Shaftoe's bright and fair,
Combing down his yellow hair;
He's my love for evermore,
    Bonny Bobby Shaftoe.

O dear, what can the matter be?
Dear, dear, what can the matter be?
O dear, what can the matter be?
  Johnny's so long at the fair.

He promised he'd buy me a fairing should please me,
And then for a kiss, oh! he vowed he would tease me,
He promised he'd bring me a bunch of blue ribbons
  To tie up my bonny brown hair.

  And it's O dear, what can the matter be?
Dear, dear, what can the matter be?
O dear, what can the matter be?
  Johnny's so long at the fair.

Hey diddle, diddle,
The cat and the fiddle,
The cow jumped over the moon;
The little dog laughed
To see such sport,
And the dish ran away with the spoon.

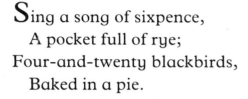

Sing a song of sixpence,
  A pocket full of rye;
Four-and-twenty blackbirds,
  Baked in a pie.

When the pie was opened,
  The birds began to sing;
Was not that a dainty dish,
  To set before the king?

The king was in his counting-house,
  Counting out his money;
The queen was in the parlour
  Eating bread and honey.

The maid was in the garden,
  Hanging out the clothes,
When down came a blackbird
  And pecked off her nose.

Happy ending.

Along came Jenny Wren
And stuck her nose back on again.

21

Mary had a little lamb,
   Its fleece was white as snow;
And everywhere that Mary went
   The lamb was sure to go.

It followed her to school one day,
   That was against the rule;
It made the children laugh and play
   To see a lamb at school.

And so the teacher turned it out,
   But still it lingered near,
And waited patiently about
   Till Mary did appear.

Why does the lamb love Mary so?
   The eager children cry;
Why, Mary loves the lamb, you know,
   The teacher did reply.

Jack and Jill
Went up the hill,
To fetch a pail of water;
Jack fell down,
And broke his crown,
And Jill came tumbling after.

Then up Jack got,
And home did trot,
As fast as he could caper;
To old Dame Dob,
Who patched his nob
With vinegar and brown paper.

23

Three little kittens
They lost their mittens,
And they began to cry,
Oh, Mother dear, we sadly fear
Our mittens we have lost.

What! lost your mittens,
You naughty kittens!
Then you shall have no pie.
  Mee-ow, mee-ow, mee-ow.
No, you shall have no pie.

The three little kittens
They found their mittens,
And they began to cry,
Oh, Mother dear,
  see here, see here,
Our mittens we have found.

Put on your mittens,
You silly kittens,
And you shall have some pie.
  Purr-r, purr-r, purr-r,
Oh, let us have some pie.

24

The three little kittens
Put on their mittens
And soon ate up the pie;
Oh, Mother dear, we greatly fear
Our mittens we have soiled.

What! soiled your mittens,
You naughty kittens!
Then they began to sigh,
    Mee-ow, mee-ow, mee-ow,
Then they began to sigh.

The three little kittens
They washed their mittens,
And hung them out to dry;
Oh, Mother dear, do you not hear,
Our mittens we have washed.

What! washed your mittens,
You good little kittens,
But I smell a rat close by.
    Mee-ow, mee-ow, mee-ow,
We smell a rat close by.

The Queen of Hearts
She made some tarts,
All on a summer's day;
The Knave of Hearts
He stole the tarts,
And took them clean away.

The King of Hearts
Called for the tarts,
And beat the knave full sore;
The Knave of Hearts
Brought back the tarts,
And vowed he'd steal no more.

Pussy cat, pussy cat,
Where have you been?
I've been to London
To look at the Queen.

Pussy cat, pussy cat,
What did you there?
I frightened a little mouse
Under her chair.

Little Bo-peep has lost her sheep,
  And can't tell where to find them;
Leave them alone and they'll come home,
  Bringing their tails behind them.

Little Bo-peep fell fast asleep,
  And dreamt she heard them bleating;
But when she awoke, she found it a joke,
  For they were still a-fleeting.

Then up she took her little crook,
  Determined for to find them;
She found them indeed,
  But it made her heart bleed,
For they'd left their tails behind them.

It happened one day, as Bo-peep did stray
  Into a meadow hard by.
There she espied their tails side by side,
  All hung on a tree to dry.

She heaved a sigh, and wiped her eye,
  And over the hillocks went rambling,
And tried what she could,
  as a shepherdess should,
To tack each again to its lambkin.

Little Miss Muffet
Sat on a tuffet,
Eating her curds and whey;
There came a big spider,
Who sat down beside her
And frightened Miss Muffet away.

Baa, baa, black sheep,
  Have you any wool?
Yes, sir, yes, sir,
  Three bags full;

One for the master,
  And one for the dame,
And one for the little boy
  Who lives down the lane.

Mary, Mary, quite contrary,
  How does your garden grow?

With silver bells and cockle shells,
  And pretty maids all in a row.

Christmas is coming,
   The geese are getting fat,
Please to put a penny
   In the old man's hat.
If you haven't got a penny,
   A ha'penny will do;
If you haven't got a ha'penny,
   Then God bless you!

Little Jack Horner
Sat in the corner,
Eating his Christmas pie;
   He put in his thumb,
   And pulled out a plum,
And said: What a good boy am I!

Jingle, bells! Jingle, bells!
   Jingle all the way;
Oh, what fun it is to ride
   In a one-horse open sleigh.

INDEX OF FIRST LINES